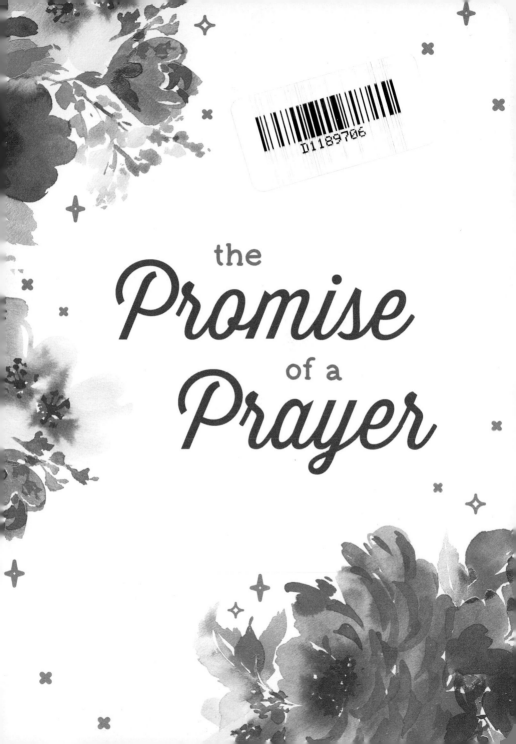

the

Promise

of a

Prayer

the Promise of a Prayer

of a

A JOURNAL TO HELP YOU GET UNSTUCK IN YOUR FAITH

BARBOUR
PUBLISHING

© 2021 by Barbour Publishing, Inc.

ISBN 978-1-64352-942-4

Text is adapted from *I Fall to My Knees* by Laura Freudig, © 2013 by Barbour Publishing, Inc. and *Everyday Moments with God* by Valorie Quesenberry, © 2012. All rights reserved.

Scripture quotations marked KJV are taken from the King James Version of the Bible.

Scripture quotations marked NIV are taken from the HOLY BIBLE, NEW INTERNATIONAL VERSION®. NIV®. Copyright © 1973, 1978, 1984, 2011 by Biblica, Inc.™ Used by permission. All rights reserved worldwide.

Scripture quotations marked NKJV are taken from the New King James Version®. Copyright © 1982 by Thomas Nelson, Inc. Used by permission. All rights reserved.

Scripture quotations marked NLT are taken from the *Holy Bible*. New Living Translation copyright© 1996, 2004, 2007, 2015 by Tyndale House Foundation. Used by permission of Tyndale House Publishers, Inc. Carol Stream, Illinois 60188. All rights reserved.

Scripture quotations marked NASB are taken from the New American Standard Bible, © 1960, 1962, 1963, 1968, 1971, 1972, 1973, 1975, 1977, 1995 by The Lockman Foundation. Used by permission.

Scripture quotations marked AMPC taken from the Amplified® Bible, Classic Edition, Copyright © 1954, 1958, 1962, 1964, 1965, 1987 by The Lockman Foundation. Used by permission. www.Lockman.org

Published by Barbour Publishing, Inc., 1810 Barbour Drive, Uhrichsville, Ohio 44683, www.barbourbooks.com

Our mission is to inspire the world with the life-changing message of the Bible.

Member of the
Evangelical Christian
Publishers Association

Printed in China.

Feeling stuck in your faith? . . .
This journal is just what you need!

This delightful prayer journal will help you in your personal faith
journey as you encounter more than 150 "Prayer Promises"
alongside related prayer starters and scripture selections.
With promises like. . .

> **Praying God's Word envelops your soul in immeasurable
> hope and comfort.**
>
> **Your prayers are a spiritual refreshing for your soul.**
>
> **The more time you spend with Jesus, the happier your
> heart will be.**
>
> **Time with the heavenly Creator can erase the doubts
> plaguing your heart.**
>
> **God is right there, in the middle of your mess.**
>
> **The Lord rejoices over you.**

. . .and plenty of room to write, you will be inspired and encouraged
to become "unstuck" in your faith and embrace the wonderful life the
heavenly Father has planned just for you!
Be blessed!

Prayer Promise #1

Prayer gives you direct access to the heavenly Father.

Father God, You are the God of the universe, and yet You ask me to come closer. I can't stand in Your presence, yet You ask me to approach with freedom and confidence. And it's all because of Jesus that I can do this! Thank You for the gift of Your Son, who allows me this access to You, my Creator. I long to know You better. Help me come to You again and again. In Jesus precious name, amen.

....

....

....

....

....

....

....

....

....

....

....

*In him and through faith in him
we may approach God with
freedom and confidence.*
EPHESIANS 3:12 NIV

Prayer Promise #2

God gives attention to your prayers.

Father, I thank You that Your ear is always listening for the prayers of Your people. You are readily listening, even for *my* voice! You know my voice from the billions of others. My words are not just spoken into empty air—no, You give them Your full attention. Forgive me for my sins today, Lord. I rest under Your mercy. Amen.

"If my people, who are called by my name, will humble themselves and pray and seek my face and turn from their wicked ways, then I will hear from heaven."
2 CHRONICLES 7:14 NIV

Prayer Promise #3

When you're exhausted and can hardly find the words, prayer is *just* what you need!

Heavenly Father, I am so very tired. I have so much to do and not nearly enough time in the day to accomplish everything. Please remind me it's in these moments that I need You most. Right here and now. Father! Lord! I want You. I need You! Please meet me here. Shower me with Your peace and comfort today. Thank You, Lord. Amen.

But to You I cry, O Lord;
and in the morning shall
my prayer come to meet You.
PSALM 88:13 AMPC

Prayer Promise #4

God will keep calling you—again and again.

Father God, I admit that sometimes I've ignored Your call. . .I've failed to come to You in prayer. Forgive me for those times. I'm grateful that You keep calling my name. Please help me to trust You enough to stop in my tracks when I hear Your voice, Lord. I am on my knees now, my Father, my King. I am listening. Amen.

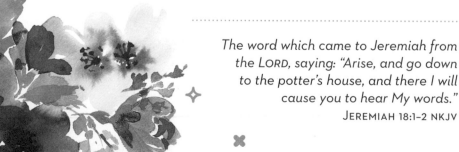

The word which came to Jeremiah from the LORD, saying: "Arise, and go down to the potter's house, and there I will cause you to hear My words."
JEREMIAH 18:1–2 NKJV

Prayer Promise #5

Prayer comes with eternal rewards.

Heavenly Father, each quiet moment in Your presence is a wonderful gift. May I never waste a second! I want to know You, Lord—growing closer to You each day—until I am called to my eternal home. Until then, I will be persistent in prayer, making time for daily conversation with You. Amen.

....

....

....

....

....

....

....

....

....

....

....

"But as for you, when you pray, go into your inner room, close your door, and pray to your Father who is in secret; and your Father who sees what is done in secret will reward you."
MATTHEW 6:6 NASB

Prayer Promise #6

God hears every word you pray.

Thank You, Father, for being the God who hears! It's mind-boggling that You know my heart even before I do! When I pray, I can trust You will answer—in Your own perfect timing. I can rest in knowing that You are answering my prayer, even *before* I pray! Amen.

....

....

....

....

....

....

....

....

....

....

....

....

....

*"Before they call I will answer; while they
are still speaking I will hear."*
ISAIAH 65:24 NIV

Prayer Promise #7

God will only provide what is within His will for you.

Lord, there are so many things I want. My wish list is quite long. Forgive me for thinking You should grant my every wish and whim. You won't give me what I want, just because I want it—instead, You'll give me only what is in line with Your will and plan for me. And for that, I thank You! Reveal Your will to me, Father. Amen.

....

....

....

....

....

....

....

....

....

....

....

Now this is the confidence that we have in Him, that if we ask anything according to His will, He hears us.
1 JOHN 5:14 NKJV

Prayer Promise #8

God is good, and He will rain down blessings on your life.

You are so good, Father! You are loving and generous. Please make Your riches visible in my life that others will see and be drawn to You. You have so much to offer, and You long to open the storehouses of heaven to each one of us. Thank You! Amen.

....

....

....

....

....

....

....

....

....

....

....

"If you, despite being evil, know how to give good gifts to your children, how much more will your Father who is in heaven give good things to those who ask Him!"
MATTHEW 7:11 NASB

Prayer Promise #9

God will shine light and love into your life—if you just ask Him to.

Father God, I long for the light of Your comforting presence. I don't want to be here alone in the dark. This world is so cold and depressing—I want to be with You, walking on streets of gold, the light of Your glory shining on my face. Please come to me, Lord. Shine Your light and love into my life in this moment. Amen.

....

....

....

....

....

....

....

....

....

....

My voice shalt thou hear in the morning, O LORD; in the morning will I direct my prayer unto thee, and will look up.
PSALM 5:3 KJV

Prayer Promise #10

When you pray, it's perfectly okay to expect a miracle.

Dear God, I come to You today, knowing You can work miracles. You heal the blind, the lame, the scarred, the leprous, the demon-possessed; You open prison cells, turn night into day, and roll up the ocean like a scroll; You bring the dead back to life. I know You love me. Please answer my prayer. Amen.

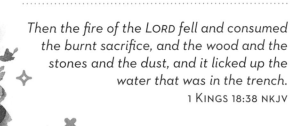

Then the fire of the LORD fell and consumed the burnt sacrifice, and the wood and the stones and the dust, and it licked up the water that was in the trench.
1 KINGS 18:38 NKJV

Prayer Promise #11

The healthiest response to fear is going to your knees in prayer.

Father God, I'm afraid of so many things—losing my health, not having enough money to pay the bills, being alone. . .just to name a few. But mostly I'm scared of not growing closer to You in this lifetime. Thank You for this fear, Lord. Remind me to give it to You—because You can handle it. . .and so much more! Amen.

*The LORD will keep you from all harm—
he will watch over your life; the LORD
will watch over your coming and
going both now and forevermore.*
PSALM 121:7–8 NIV

Prayer Promise #12

The best way to live your life is with a heart perfectly in tune with God's will.

Lord, You gave me life, and I praise You! Forgive me for not always loving and appreciating this body that You've given me—it truly is an amazing creation and wonderful gift. Today, Lord, I want to talk to You just as I breathe—in and out, all day long. Fill my mouth with Your praise. Let my lips always be whispering Your name. Amen.

Rejoice always, pray without ceasing.
1 THESSALONIANS 5:16–17 NASB

Prayer Promise #13

The heavenly Father knows everything.

Lord of the universe, You know everything; You see everything; You are everywhere; You are eternal. And You long to teach us everything. . .we only need to read Your Word and spend time with You. So I yield my heart and my mind to You, Father. Amen.

"Call to me and I will answer you and tell you great and unsearchable things you do not know."
JEREMIAH 33:3 NIV

Prayer Promise #14

God will give you wisdom freely and generously.

Father God, I sometimes feel led to step into potentially sticky situations—especially when someone I love might be in trouble. But I know that stepping into a mess without Your blessing will only make things worse. I want to be used by You in people's lives. But first, I need Your wisdom. Thank You that You promise to give it to me in abundance. Amen.

If any of you lacks wisdom, let him ask of God, who gives to all liberally and without reproach, and it will be given to him.
JAMES 1:5 NKJV

Prayer Promise #15

God is patient.

Heavenly Father, I'm not patient about waiting for things I want to happen . . .right now! But You are so very patient with me and others. You won't return until *everyone* has heard the Gospel. Thank You that Your incredible patience and love are greater than our persistent sin. Please lead me to share Your truth with someone who needs to hear it today, Lord. Amen.

....

....

....

....

....

....

....

....

....

....

....

For I am not ashamed of the gospel of Christ: for it is the power of God unto salvation to every one that believeth.
ROMANS 1:16 KJV

Prayer Promise #16

Praying God's Word envelops your soul in immeasurable hope and comfort.

Lord, I can do *all things* through You! You offer me strength that I can't find anywhere else. Thank You, Father, for Your Word that speaks to me so perfectly in my time of need. No other book can offer that! I need Your Word today. Help me to pray the words right back to You—all day long. Amen.

....

....

....

....

....

....

....

....

....

....

....

I can do all things through Christ who strengthens me.
PHILIPPIANS 4:13 NKJV

Prayer Promise #17

Prayer can help grow you into the wonderful human God created you to be.

God, I know I am a work in progress—Your work, to be exact! I am not even close to becoming who I want to be, Lord. And I'm certainly not who You want me to be right now. But still You love me! Thank You for Your mercy today and for Your promise that You are carrying out Your good work in me. Amen.

....

....

....

....

....

....

....

....

....

....

....

....

Being confident of this, that he who began a good work in you will carry it on to completion until the day of Christ Jesus.
PHILIPPIANS 1:6 NIV

Prayer Promise #18

God will provide the strength you need to deal with skeptics.

Lord, since I've come to know You, I've had encounters with my fair share of skeptics. Nothing I say seems to make any difference in their opinion of You—and I grow weary in the process. Please give me the strength to keep trying, lovingly and gently, to pry them loose from the lies they are holding on to. You are my Rock. Amen.

....

....

....

....

....

....

....

....

....

*For the Word that God speaks is alive
and full of power. . .it is sharper than
any two-edged sword, penetrating to
the dividing line of the breath of life
(soul) and [the immortal] spirit.*
HEBREWS 4:12 AMPC

Prayer Promise #19

When you don't have the words to pray, the Holy Spirit does!

Father God, my mind and my heart feel empty right now. And I don't know how—or what—to pray. You already know I am weak and wordless in this moment. Thank You for Your Spirit, my Comforter, who speaks for me during these times. Amen.

....

....

....

....

....

....

....

....

....

....

So too the [Holy] Spirit comes to our aid and bears us up in our weakness; for we do not know what prayer to offer nor how to offer it worthily as we ought, but the Spirit Himself goes to meet our supplication and pleads in our behalf with unspeakable yearnings and groanings too deep for utterance.
ROMANS 8:26 AMPC

Prayer Promise #20

Jesus makes His home in your heart.

Lord, I am so thankful that You promise never to leave me or forsake me. Because of the great gift of Your Spirit, I know I am not alone. Thank You for making Your home in my heart. You are my Comforter and Strength—You're all I'll ever need. Amen.

....

....

....

....

....

....

....

....

....

....

And I will ask the Father, and He will give you another Comforter (Counselor, Helper, Intercessor, Advocate, Strengthener, and Standby), that He may remain with you forever.
JOHN 14:16 AMPC

Prayer Promise #21

You'll encounter Christ's powerful presence
when you approach Him in quietness and rest.

Father, there are so many things to do—and never enough time to accomplish it all. The noise and busyness of life is unending. Yet You call me to come away, just as Jesus did, in quietness and rest. Thank You for wanting to protect my heart in this crazy, demanding world. Amen.

....

....

....

....

....

....

....

....

....

....

....

*For thus saith the Lord GOD, the Holy
One of Israel; In returning and rest
shall ye be saved; in quietness and
in confidence shall be your strength.*
ISAIAH 30:15 KJV

Prayer Promise #22

Because of Jesus, every day is a reason to celebrate!

Forgive me, Father. I so often walk around with a long face, complaining about this and that. But Your Word calls me to do otherwise: eat good food, drink, share with others. . . From the moment You sent Your Son to earth, every day should be a celebration. And You offer strength through joy! Thank You. Amen.

....

....

....

....

....

....

....

....

....

....

Nehemiah said, "Go and enjoy choice food and sweet drinks, and send some to those who have nothing prepared. This day is holy to our Lord. Do not grieve, for the joy of the LORD is your strength."
NEHEMIAH 8:10 NIV

Prayer Promise #23

Your prayers are a spiritual refreshing for your soul.

Jesus, You are the living water. Your Word says that if I come to You, streams of living water will flow from within me. Thank You for this promise. When my soul feels empty and dry, I only need to enter Your heavenly presence—and I will find the refreshing I need. Amen.

....

....

....

....

....

....

....

....

....

....

On the last and greatest day of the festival, Jesus stood and said in a loud voice, "Let anyone who is thirsty come to me and drink. Whoever believes in me, as Scripture has said, rivers of living water will flow from within them."
JOHN 7:37–38 NIV

Prayer Promise #24

God can—and will—use His followers to influence other believers.

Father God, thank You for speaking to us through our fellow believers. They can help us find joy, comfort, peace, love, wisdom, and understanding right when we need those things the most. And You, Father, are the One who sends them to our rescue. What a blessing! Amen.

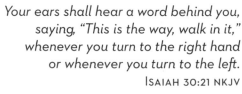

Your ears shall hear a word behind you, saying, "This is the way, walk in it," whenever you turn to the right hand or whenever you turn to the left.
ISAIAH 30:21 NKJV

Prayer Promise #25

**Reading God's Word and spending quiet time
in prayer is like sitting at Jesus' feet.**

Dear Jesus, Mary and Martha's house must have been a place of comfort, rest, and welcome for You. How I wish I could sit at Your feet like Mary did. . .but then I realize that when I open Your Word and spend time in Your presence, I am! My heart is a welcome place for You, Father. Amen.

*"Martha, Martha," the Lord answered, "you
are worried and upset about many things,
but few things are needed—or indeed only
one. Mary has chosen what is better, and
it will not be taken away from her."*
LUKE 10:41–42 NIV

Prayer Promise #26

The more time you spend with Jesus, the happier your heart will be.

Today I choose joy, Lord. Despite my less-than-perfect circumstances, I will choose to take whatever You give with open arms. I will pray continually as I go about my day; I will meditate on Your holy Word in any and every situation. This quality time with You will lead me to joy! Amen.

All the days of the afflicted are evil, but he who is of a merry heart has a continual feast.
PROVERBS 15:15 NKJV

Prayer Promise #27

God wants you to let go of your own agenda and give Him complete control.

Father, I admit I spend a lot of time trying to control situations and even other people. This is all futile and only leads to anxiety for me. Remind me that I can only control my own heart—and this is only because of Your grace and the gift of Your Spirit. Work on me and through me, Lord. Amen.

All the ways of a man are pure in his own eyes, but the LORD weighs the spirits. Commit your works to the LORD, and your thoughts will be established.
PROVERBS 16:2–3 NKJV

Prayer Promise #28

Our words should glorify the Savior—always.

Heavenly Father, my life is full of words—both written and spoken. I am bombarded by them all day long—through books, television, movies, neighbors, family, friends, letters, email, advertisements, and radio. Yet I don't often stop to think about whether they glorify You. And that is my true desire: to glorify You, Lord. Please help only praiseworthy words flow from me. Thank You! Amen.

As newborn babes, desire the pure milk of the word, that you may grow thereby, if indeed you have tasted that the Lord is gracious.
1 PETER 2: 2–3 NKJV

Prayer Promise #29

Jesus offers hope and healing for your hurting heart.

Lord, I sometimes find myself obsessing over my hurts and hang-ups. When this is where my focus lies, my wounds only become deeper and my heart sadder. Remind me that by doing this, I am pushing You away. I am not welcoming Your forgiveness and healing. Please forgive me. I want to know You, Lord, and Your saving power. Amen.

....

....

....

....

....

....

....

....

....

....

....

....

He heals the brokenhearted
and binds up their wounds.
PSALM 147:3 NASB

Prayer Promise #30

When you enter the presence of the Savior, you will find rest for your soul.

Father, my cares in this world are heavy and burdensome. But no matter what is happening in my life, I know this: You are good! You are holy! And You are God! Remind me of Your goodness. . .of Your unending love and mercy. Help me to speak (and think) words of pure joy! Amen.

"Come to Me, all who are weary and burdened, and I will give you rest. Take My yoke upon you and learn from Me, for I am gentle and humble in heart, and You will find rest for your souls."
MATTHEW 11:28–29 NASB

Prayer Promise #31

God knows your hidden wounds better than you do.

Dear Lord, it's human nature to let my hidden hurts bleed onto others. But this only creates further hurt and destruction. I am so thankful that You know me better than I even know myself. You are the great Healer, Father. You can heal with a simple touch. . .with a brief word. You heal with Your presence. Show me my hurts, Lord. Heal me. Amen.

Therefore, if anyone is in Christ,
the new creation has come:
The old has gone, the new is here!
2 CORINTHIANS 5:17 NIV

Prayer Promise #32

The Lord's ways are higher than Yours—
He knows exactly what you need.

I admit. . .rest doesn't come easily to me, Father. I am more often a human "do"-ing than a human "be"-ing. But Your ways are higher than mine. I trust You to show me just what I need and when I need it. Help me to recognize when I need rest, Lord. And show me what true rest is. Amen.

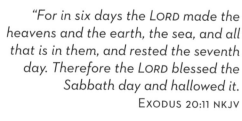

"For in six days the LORD made the heavens and the earth, the sea, and all that is in them, and rested the seventh day. Therefore the LORD blessed the Sabbath day and hallowed it.
EXODUS 20:11 NKJV

Prayer Promise #33

The heavenly Father is always right by your side—even when He seems far away.

Father, at times I've woken with a solution to my problem—one that seemed to appear from nowhere. I realize those answers came from You. Thank You, Lord, for counseling me in the night. . .for instructing me even when I'm unaware of Your presence. The reality of Your nearness brings me comfort. Thank You. Amen.

I will praise the LORD, who counsels me;
even at night my heart instructs me.
PSALM 16:7 NIV

Prayer Promise #34

Time with the heavenly Creator can erase the doubts plaguing your heart.

Lord, my mind often gets carried away with doubts and unease. Those rogue thoughts can quickly turn into bitterness and despair. I even find myself questioning, *Lord, are You there? Do You really love me?* . . . Help to ease my troubled mind. Give me the diligence I am lacking—so I can grow my roots deep into Your streams of living water. Amen.

....
....
....
....
....
....
....
....
....
....
....
....

A man is not established by wickedness, but the root of the righteous cannot be moved.
PROVERBS 12:3 NKJV

Prayer Promise #35

The heavenly Father provides strength so you can stand through life's hardships.

God, I will wholly rely on You in life's difficult seasons. When hard times come, I'm unable to stand on my own strength—but with You holding me up, I can! No matter what happens in my story, Father, I know without a doubt that I will look back from heaven one day and say, "Hallelujah! Hallelujah!" Amen.

....

....

....

....

....

....

....

....

....

....

And we know that all things work together for good to them that love God, to them who are the called according to his purpose.
ROMANS 8:28 KJV

Prayer Promise #36

God and His Word will illuminate the darkness in your life.

Gracious heavenly Father, You are so very good. When my life becomes dark with sin and the unknown, I can reach up to You. . .and You will illuminate my world. You bring comfort and light into my life like nothing else can. You are present. You are real. I praise You, Lord! Amen.

The entrance and unfolding of Your words give light; their unfolding gives understanding (discernment and comprehension) to the simple.
PSALM 119:130 AMPC

Prayer Promise #37

Your true home is in heaven.

Dear heavenly Father, moving is always stressful. But no matter where my earthly address may be, I know You will be there to love me and care for me. . .to comfort me. Help me keep my eyes focused on You and You alone. Remind me that my true home is in heaven and my true roots in You, Father. Amen.

....
....
....
....
....
....
....
....
....
....

Instead, they were longing for a better country—a heavenly one. Therefore God is not ashamed to be called their God, for he has prepared a city for them.
HEBREWS 11:16 NIV

Prayer Promise #38

The heavenly Father longs to see your arms lifted in praise.

God, praising You feels so wonderful. It refreshes my soul—like a plant after a much-needed spring rain. I praise You for the beauty of the earth, the skies, the heavens, and for Your great love. . .which surrounds and sustains it all. Amen.

....

....

....

....

....

....

....

....

....

....

....

He dawns on them like the morning light when the sun rises on a cloudless morning, when the tender grass springs out of the earth through clear shining after rain.
2 SAMUEL 23:4 AMPC

Prayer Promise #39

The courage you need to stay on the right path comes from God and God alone.

Father God, today I ask for courage. I need Your strength to help me break old sinful habits that hold me back from the freedom You promise. Help me to recognize that even if it looks like I'm the only one following this path, You are leading me every step of the way. And You, Father, can be trusted! Amen.

....

....

....

....

....

....

....

....

....

....

By faith Abraham obeyed when he was called to go out to the place which he would receive as an inheritance. And he went out, not knowing where he was going.
HEBREWS 11:8 NKJV

Prayer Promise #40

You are safe and secure with Christ.

Lord, when the wind whips and howls, I am reminded of my own frailty. And I wonder how long I can hold on in life's storms. How many more tragedies, trials, and temptations can I take? But You are here with me through it all, beloved Savior. Your everlasting arms are around me—comforting, sustaining, protecting. Thank You. Amen.

The eternal God is your refuge and dwelling place, and underneath are the everlasting arms.
DEUTERONOMY 33:27 AMPC

Prayer Promise #41

The heavenly Father has gifted you—and your brothers and sisters in Christ—for service.

Lord, I am so thankful for my church. I am thankful for my brothers and sisters who are my extended family because of our shared faith. Thank You for gifting each one of us in unique ways. Please bless all those who serve in our churches, communities, and beyond. Give them extra measures of Your joy, strength, comfort, and love. Amen.

....

....

....

....

....

....

....

....

....

There are different kinds of gifts,
but the same Spirit distributes them.
There are different kinds of service,
but the same Lord. There are different
kinds of working, but in all of them and
in everyone it is the same God at work.
1 CORINTHIANS 12:4–6 NIV

Prayer Promise #42

God is right there, in the middle of your mess.

I am so thankful, Father, that You're not afraid of messes. You will reach right into the tangles and the mire. The beauty of it all is that You can see beyond my mess—and right into my heart. I want to be more like You, Lord. I want to love others in—and through—their messes too. Amen.

....

....

....

....

....

....

....

....

....

....

....

....

....

*For the Son of man is come to seek
and to save that which was lost.*
LUKE 19:10 KJV

Prayer Promise #43

The Lord rejoices over you.

Father, I enjoy the little birds that frequent my garden—the chickadees, the robins, the juncos, the purple finches. I praise You for their glorious songs! Help me to remember that as much as I rejoice in songbirds, You rejoice in me even more. Thank You! Amen.

*"The LORD your God in your midst,
the Mighty One, will save; He will
rejoice over you with gladness,
He will quiet you with His love,
He will rejoice over you with singing."*
ZEPHANIAH 3:17 NKJV

Prayer Promise #44

Your mind can't fully comprehend the greatness of God.

Lord, You are infinite. . .beyond my comprehension. Infinity is such a non-human sort of concept—and so I try to think about how big You really are, but my mind keeps trying to reduce You to something smaller that I *can* understand. I praise You, Father, that You are wholly infinite and infinitely holy. There is none like You. Amen.

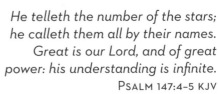

He telleth the number of the stars;
he calleth them all by their names.
Great is our Lord, and of great
power: his understanding is infinite.
PSALM 147:4–5 KJV

Prayer Promise #45

God gives you grace in the unknown.

Father, when I'm reeling from loss, I find myself confused—even though You provide me with comfort and truth. I still find myself asking, "Why?" Because there is so much I don't understand. . .so much I don't know. I rest in Your sovereignty, Lord. Please provide me with grace in the not-knowing. Amen.

So when. . .this mortal has put on immortality, then shall be brought to pass the saying that is written: "Death is swallowed up in victory."
1 Corinthians 15:54 NKJV

Prayer Promise #46

God is your Rescuer.

Father God, when I think about all You've done for me, it moves me to tears. I was lost and alone and enslaved by this sin-stricken world. . .and You came. You rescued me. You made a way for my freedom. There is no one who loves me like You, Lord. Thank You! Amen.

....
....
....
....
....
....
....
....
....
....
....

"He rescues and he saves;
he performs signs and wonders
in the heavens and on the earth."
Daniel 6:27 niv

Prayer Promise #47

Your heavenly Father is the ultimate Surprise-Giver.

Lord, You never fail to surprise me at the many ways You love me. Thank You for the way rain droplets decorate a branch like hundreds of tiny diamonds. Thank You for an unexpected smile from a stranger. Thank You for pictures You paint with every evening sunset. Thank You for delighting me with the beauty of Your Word and Your world. Amen.

For the LORD thy God bringeth thee into a good land, a land of brooks of water, of fountains and depths that spring out of valleys and hills.
DEUTERONOMY 8:7 KJV

Prayer Promise #48

In the hardship, Christ is your hope.

Father, I am saddened by the horrors of the world that happen right alongside its beauty. It's so hard to know how to handle it all. And so I cry out to You—the Hope-Giver. You alone provide all the love and comfort my soul will ever need. Thank You for loving me. Amen.

....

....

....

....

....

....

....

....

....

....

....

....

....

"Though he slay me,
yet will I hope in him."
JOB 13:15 NIV

Prayer Promise #49

There is transformative power in the love of Jesus.

In moments of deep distress, Lord, You reach down and pull me from the pit. Scriptures, people, hymn lyrics, moments of unexpected beauty. . . they all show me that You are right there with me—loving me, lifting me. Thank You for the delight and wonder You add to my story—for giving me so much to share with others. Thank You for the transformative power of Your love. Amen.

*He also brought me up out of a horrible pit.
. . . He has put a new song in my mouth—
praise to our God; many will see it and
fear, and will trust in the LORD.*
PSALM 40:2–3 NKJV

Prayer Promise #50

God's love has the power to move mountains and calm storms.

Father, I admit I don't often think about the word "love" and what it really means—how much power it holds. Your love can move mountains, heal the blind and sick, calm raging storms, and redeem sinners like me. Our earthly love is only a dim shadow of what You feel for Your children. I love You, Lord. Amen.

....

....

....

....

....

....

....

....

....

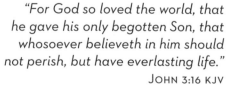

"For God so loved the world, that he gave his only begotten Son, that whosoever believeth in him should not perish, but have everlasting life."
JOHN 3:16 KJV

Prayer Promise #51

Humanity is just one prayer away from eternity.

Father, I am surrounded on all sides by people who are dangerously close to spending eternity without You. Open my eyes to the opportunities You present to me—moments when I can speak wisdom into the lives of those who don't yet know You. You love each human being on this planet so much, Father. And each is just a prayer away from an eternity so wonderful they can't even begin to imagine. Amen.

....

....

....

....

....

....

....

....

....

Who is a God like You, who pardons wrongdoing and passes over a rebellious act of the remnant of His possession? He does not retain His anger forever, because He delights in mercy.
MICAH 7:18 NASB

Prayer Promise #52

One touch from Jesus offers complete cleansing.

Lord, day after day, I'm astounded by Your love—a love so great that You willingly left Your kingly throne to come down into the muck and sin of this world. I am often missing the love, joy, peace, patience, kindness, goodness, faithfulness, gentleness, and self-control that are my birthright in Christ. And yet, You are willing to reach out and touch me, cleansing me with Your amazing love. Thank You. Amen.

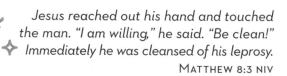

Jesus reached out his hand and touched the man. "I am willing," he said. "Be clean!" Immediately he was cleansed of his leprosy.
MATTHEW 8:3 NIV

Prayer Promise #53

God is the ultimate Promise-Keeper.

Heavenly Father, I've made many promises in my lifetime. And while I'd like to say I've kept every single one, we both know that isn't true. Forgive me for each broken promise. You, Lord, are One who keeps His promises, who remains faithful from generation to generation. Teach me what it means to be truly faithful. Amen.

For no matter how many promises God has made, they are "Yes" in Christ.
2 CORINTHIANS 1:20 NIV

Prayer Promise #54

The King of kings put aside His crown to become one of us.

You, Father, are Lord of the universe, yet You left Your throne and came to earth to be near us. You are the giver and sustainer of life, yet You sacrificed Your Son to save us. You are the King of kings, yet You put aside Your crown to become one of us. What You sacrificed for me—and all of humanity—makes no earthly sense. But You did it, and I am forever grateful. Amen.

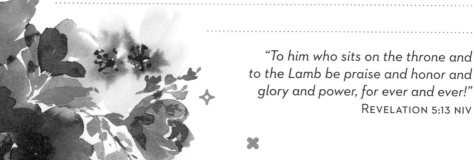

"To him who sits on the throne and to the Lamb be praise and honor and glory and power, for ever and ever!"
REVELATION 5:13 NIV

Prayer Promise #55

You are complete in Christ.

Lord, I confess that I often equate physical contentment with spiritual health. This isn't necessarily true, according to Your Word. The truth is this: I am complete in You, regardless of any circumstance. Help me to live in the light of eternity, unswayed by my finances, health, or other events that might attempt to distract me from You. Amen.

....

....

....

....

....

....

....

....

....

....

....

From the fruit of their mouth a person's stomach is filled; with the harvest of their lips they are satisfied.
PROVERBS 18:20 NIV

Prayer Promise #56

There is a God-shaped hole in every human being that only He can fill.

Thank You, Father God, for finding me. . .for drawing me into a relationship with You. When I asked You to become Lord of my life, the piece that had been forever missing—that hole I had tried to fill with worldly things—suddenly clicked into place. Thank You, Lord, for showing me I was created for something other than a "normal" life. Life with You is *always* an adventure. Amen.

Once you were alienated from God. . . .
But now he has reconciled you by Christ's
physical body through death to present
you holy in his sight, without blemish
and free from accusation.
COLOSSIANS 1:21–22 NIV

Prayer Promise #57

God calls you to greater faith.

Father, when I stand before You, what will You say? . . . I know You certainly won't judge me based on the merit of others. It won't matter whether I was married to a Bible scholar or that my cousin was a missionary. No— You'll only see *me*. And, Father, how I long to hear You say, "Well done." Increase my faith and devotion to You. Amen.

....

....

....

....

....

....

....

....

....

....

....

*"But rise and stand on your feet; for I
have appeared to you for this purpose,
to make you a minister and a witness."*
ACTS 26:16 NKJV

Prayer Promise #58

To be saved, only one thing is necessary: Believe in the Lord Jesus!

Lord, I have a tendency to add human rules to the simplicity of the Gospel. Which Bible version is superior to others? Maybe some people should dress differently? Or speak with a special "Christian" vocabulary? But Your Word says this: believe in the Lord Jesus Christ, and you will be saved. Nothing more, nothing less. Help me to stay true to Your simple truth. Amen.

They replied, "Believe in the Lord Jesus, and you will be saved—you and your household."

ACTS 16:31 NIV

Prayer Promise #59

God's love can't be earned—it's a beautiful gift!

Father, I admit that I often base my worth on how much I am able to accomplish in a day. Please remind me that I can never do enough to earn Your love or approval. This is because I am already completely and eternally loved by You. The only payment that needed to be made was done by the sacrifice on the cross. And for that, I thank You, Lord. Amen.

The LORD appeared to long ago, saying, "I have loved you with an everlasting love; therefore I have drawn you out with kindness."
JEREMIAH 31:3 NASB

Prayer Promise #60

God is never too busy for you.

I am so thankful that You're never too busy to listen to my thoughts and concerns, Father. The only thing that keeps my prayers from reaching You is my own unconfessed sin. Help me examine my heart when it seems like I'm experiencing Your silence. Forgive me. I long to stand before You, complete and unashamed. Amen.

"Then you call on the name of your god, and I will call on the name of the LORD. The god who answers by fire—he is God."

1 KINGS 18:24 NIV

Prayer Promise #61

God will carry every burden
so you don't have to.

Thank You, Father, for helping me realize that I have two choices: I can either choose to carry burdens all by myself; or I can lay them at the foot of the cross, and You'll take care of them. And when I give my troubles and worries to You, I get a double blessing because You'll replace them with joy. What a delightful tradeoff! Thank You, Lord! Amen.

If we confess our sins, he is faithful
and just to forgive us our sins, and to
cleanse us from all unrighteousness.
1 JOHN 1:9 KJV

Prayer Promise #62

God knows just what you need.

I know You are the giver of good gifts, Father. But I'm often convinced that I need more—so many of my "wants" seem so nice and necessary. Thank You for the things I have. . .and help me control my desire for more stuff. No "thing" will ever satisfy me or make me complete. Only You can do that, Lord. Amen.

I will be fully satisfied as with the richest of foods; with singing lips my mouth will praise you.
PSALM 63:5 NIV

Prayer Promise #63

The heavenly Father
is 100% perfect.

You are so wonderful and perfect, Father, that I can't even begin to imagine it. No matter how I strive to be and do better, I will never achieve perfection. Please help me to accept and be content with that. Only You are perfect—and I am complete now in You. Amen.

....

....

....

....

....

....

....

....

....

....

....

....

....

As for God, His way is perfect.
2 SAMUEL 22:31 AMPC

Prayer Promise #64

God speaks to your heart through His Word.

Father God, I ask for insight as I read Your Word. Reveal Your Spirit to me. I want to know You better today than I did yesterday—and I can accomplish that by spending time with You and in the Bible. Thank You for the verses I will read today and how they will speak to me—as if You wrote them for me just this morning. Amen.

I lean on, rely on, and trust in Your word.
PSALM 119:42 AMPC

Prayer Promise #65

**The heavenly Father is molding you
into the person He created you to be.**

Lord, I confess that sadly, I often spend more time worrying about what others think of me than what You must think. I'm so sorry. You made me just like this—for Your good purposes. Help me trust that You are molding this lump of clay into something precious in Your sight. Thank You, Father. Amen.

*I will praise You, for I am fearfully
and wonderfully made.*
PSALM 139:14 NKJV

Prayer Promise #66

**You can trust God to lead you
to those who need to know Him.**

Lord, the people who need You—and who are actively looking for You—don't usually advertise it out loud. And often, these people really do look like they have it all together. . .like their lives are perfect. I need Your eyes, Father, to see exactly where and how I can reach out to these unbelievers. Help me to love them as You love them. Amen.

In Him you have been made complete.
COLOSSIANS 2:10 NASB

Prayer Promise #67

It's imperative that you become a prayer warrior.

Heavenly Father, I know I've been surrounded by loving Christ-followers who have prayed for me from the moment I arrived in this world. And I am so thankful for them. Please bless these people today and strengthen their faith in the invisible power of their work. Thank You for all faithful prayer warriors. Help me to become a faithful prayer warrior too. Amen.

. . . .

. . . .

. . . .

. . . .

. . . .

. . . .

. . . .

. . . .

. . . .

. . . .

. . . .

Always labouring fervently for you in prayers, that ye may stand perfect and complete in all the will of God.
COLOSSIANS 4:12 KJV

Prayer Promise #68

You are complete in Christ Jesus.

What does it really mean to be complete, Lord? Whole. Absolute. Total. Finished. Accomplished. Concluded. Fulfilled. Done. If I'm complete in You, Father, then there is nothing more that needs to be done. All the work was completed at the cross. For this, I am so thankful and I praise You! Amen.

But we all, with unveiled faces, looking as in a mirror at the glory of the Lord, are being transformed into the same image from glory to glory.
2 CORINTHIANS 3:18 NASB

Prayer Promise #69

God has breathed a spark of creativity into your soul.

Sometimes I fear my well of creativity has run dry, Lord. But then I remember that You created everything out of nothing! You simply spoke, and it came to be. You are the Author of life, the Word made flesh. Thank You for breathing that same spark of creativity into me. I know that if I keep my eyes fixed on You, my creativity will overflow—there is no end to the ways I can praise You! Amen.

....

....

....

....

....

....

....

....

....

....

....

*"Whoever drinks the water I give them
will never thirst. Indeed, the water I give
them will become in them a spring of
water welling up to eternal life."*
JOHN 4:14 NIV

Prayer Promise #70

God wants you to slow down and enjoy life's little moments.

Heavenly Father, I have so much to do every day and so little time to get it done. I feel like I'm always running behind. I know this isn't what You want for my life. May I learn from Jesus, who was never in a hurry—always taking time to pray on a mountainside or chat beside a well. Give me wisdom as I set aside my demanding to-do list for Your holy will. Amen.

There is a time for everything,
and a season for every
activity under the heavens.
ECCLESIASTES 3:1 NIV

Prayer Promise #71

The heavenly Father wants you to prioritize your relationships.

Lord, You know how often selfishness, angry words, hurt feelings, and laziness damage my relationships with friends and family. But please know that I love You and am learning from Your example to love others well. Increase my love; make it shine out for everyone to see. Make me a light on a hill, Father. Thank You. Amen.

....

....

....

....

....

....

....

....

....

....

....

No one has seen God at any time.
If we love one another, God abides in us,
and His love has been perfected in us.
1 JOHN 4:12 NKJV

Prayer Promise #72

God wants to help calm the chaos in your life.

Father God, I feel so good when I have my life in order. But when chaos reigns, it's a different story: I feel scattered, bewildered, short-tempered. Help me to remember that it's no different with my spiritual life. Help me to keep the cobwebs and confusion in check with daily conversations with You, Bible study, and meditation on Your Word. Thank You! Amen.

You will keep him in perfect peace,
whose mind is stayed on You.
Isaiah 26:3 NKJV

Prayer Promise #73

**God places people in your life to hold you
accountable for your choices and actions.**

Heavenly Father, thank You for the reminder that I am fully capable of any
sin. I know the temptations will come. Please protect me, Lord. Surround
me with people who will ask tough questions about my life and hold me
accountable. I want to be used by You. Amen.

....

....

....

....

....

....

....

....

....

....

....

....

....

*The LORD will be at your side and will
keep your foot from being snared.*
PROVERBS 3:26 NIV

Prayer Promise #74

Your heavenly Father will help you to bloom.

When I feel small and insignificant, Father, You remind me that You make everything beautiful in Your perfect timing. You never fail to remind me where true worth lies. Thank You for the contentment that only comes from You. I love You and trust You completely. If my heart is set on You, then You will give me the desires of my heart. Amen.

He hath made every thing beautiful in his time.
ECCLESIASTES 3:11 KJV

Prayer Promise #75

**Where believers gather,
Christ is present among them.**

Father, thank You for allowing me to be part of the most amazing thing in the world—Your Church. Wherever and whenever we gather together, You are there. And Your glory is made visible. Help me to see the Church with Your eyes. I want to see just as You do. Amen.

....

....

....

....

....

....

....

....

....

....

....

*For now we see through a glass,
darkly; but then face to face:
now I know in part; but then shall
I know even as also I am known.*
1 CORINTHIANS 13:12 KJV

Prayer Promise #76

Even in your trials, God deserves your praise.

Father God, I have never felt the terror of a mob; I have never been brutalized, beaten, or imprisoned for my beliefs. My trials are fairly ordinary. . . and for that, I am so very thankful. Even still, I have challenges that make finding words of praise quite difficult. I want to be faithful to praise You in every circumstance, Father. Please help me in my struggles. Amen.

Rejoice to the extent that you partake of Christ's sufferings, that when His glory is revealed, you may also be glad with exceeding joy.
1 PETER 4:13 NKJV

Prayer Promise #77

**Spending time with God will help
you sort through culture's confusion.**

Father, I can be gullible at times. More than I'd like to admit, in fact. From the very beginning of creation, humans were tricked and led astray. And I am no different. I need you every moment, Lord, to help me sort through the confusion in my mind so I can be certain of the truth—of everything that glorifies You. Amen.

*"Then you will know the truth,
and the truth will set you free."*
JOHN 8:32 NIV

Prayer Promise #78

The Lord often turns the ordinary into the extraordinary.

Heavenly Father, thank You for the example of Mary—an ordinary girl from nowhere special. And yet. . .You chose her to become the mother of Jesus. She was humble and faithful to You. Only You, Lord, delight in turning our expectations on their head in such surprising ways. Help me to be more like Mary, and say continually, "Let it be to me according to Your Word." Amen.

"For He who is mighty has done great things for me, and holy is His name."
LUKE 1:49 NKJV

Prayer Promise #79

With the heavenly Father's help, you can forgive any offense.

Father, forgiveness is so hard. It seems easier to hold on to my resentment. Help me, Lord. Any time I lay my burden at the cross, I feel like a heavy weight has been lifted. But I sometimes find myself coming back to the burden and picking it up all over again. I am looking to You, Lord. Help me to forgive—help me to be more like You. Amen.

....

....

....

....

....

....

....

....

....

....

....

"Forgive, and you will be forgiven."
LUKE 6:37 NIV

Prayer Promise #80

**Praying for your enemies brings
hope and healing to your soul.**

Heavenly Father, Your Word instructs us to pray for our enemies. And
though this is a difficult thing to do, it certainly works. When I pray for
someone I don't like—or even someone who just annoys me—I begin to
experience more positive feelings. It's amazing what happens when I lift
a difficult human being up to You, Lord. This is proof that when I obey
Your Word, I can feel Your power at work in me! Amen.

*"But I tell you, love your enemies and pray
for those who persecute you, that you may
be children of your Father in heaven."*
MATTHEW 5:44–45 NIV

Prayer Promise #81

Your heavenly Creator will never give up on you!

Heavenly Father, I am often slow to learn the lessons You are trying to teach me. But You are patient. . .You are loving. . .You are willing to wait for me to catch on—and You refuse to turn Your back on me. Although it might take longer than I'd like, I *will* get there, Lord. And I trust that You will be there waiting for me, encouraging me, and giving me strength. Thank You! Amen.

You are from God, little children, and have overcome them; because greater is He who is in you than he who is in the world.
1 JOHN 4:4 NASB

Prayer Promise #82

The heavenly Father is all you'll ever need. . .He is enough.

Lord, when I think about all the stuff I have, it's embarrassing to admit that I still want more. Another outfit to jam into my already-packed closet, the newest electronic gadget, a house with a pool. . .it never stops. Remind me, Father, that only You can fill the hole that I try to fill with more stuff. Thank You for providing everything I'll ever need. Amen.

....

....

....

....

....

....

....

....

....

....

....

....

*But godliness with
contentment is great gain.*
1 TIMOTHY 6:6 KJV

Prayer Promise #83

The Lord has placed the power of influence in you.

Father, I feel so insignificant at times. . .like I really don't matter all that much. But the truth is that everyone who follows You has influence—in every big and small circle they move in—and yes, that includes me! Thank You for empowering me, Lord. I will use my influence to reach everyone I can for You! Amen.

....

....

....

....

....

....

....

....

....

....

*"You did not choose me, but I chose you
and appointed you so that you might go
and bear fruit—fruit that will last."*
JOHN 15:16 NIV

Prayer Promise #84

God created everything from nothing.

Father, it never ceases to amaze me how people try to explain life apart from You. No matter what theories circulate, I believe You alone are the Master Creator. I believe You created everything from nothing. I believe You spoke light and life into existence. Apart from You, this complex, detailed universe wouldn't exist. Thank You for Your beautifully amazing creation. Amen.

Then God said, "Let there be light"; and there was light. God saw that the light was good; and God separated the light from the darkness.
GENESIS 1:3–4 NASB

Prayer Promise #85

Nothing on this earth compares to heaven.

Father God, this world is so beautiful and so very large. I wish I could travel to all the destinations on my wish list; however, it's just not possible for me in this lifetime. Thank You, Lord, for reminding me that even though I can't see all the wonders of the world, I won't be missing a thing—because heaven is the ultimate destination. In heaven, no one—including me!—will want for anything left behind. Thank You. Amen.

....

....

....

....

....

....

....

....

....

....

*Now faith is the certainty of things
hoped for, a proof of things not seen.*
HEBREWS 11:1 NASB

Prayer Promise #86

God is the ultimate Healer of sin.

Father, none of us will ever be free from sin—not this side of heaven. Sin is a disease that affects every human being—but the good news is there is hope for healing because of the gift of Your Son! One day, sin will be obliterated, and all who believe in You will spend eternity in heaven. Thank You for providing the way to complete freedom from sin, Father. Amen.

Confess your sins to each other and pray for each other so that you may be healed. The earnest prayer of a righteous person has great power and produces wonderful results.
JAMES 5:16 NLT

Prayer Promise #87

The heavenly Father makes all things new—including you.

Heavenly Father, I'm not getting any younger. Each time I look in the mirror, I see new lines on my face, more wiry gray hairs. . .and I wonder, *Am I really fearfully and wonderfully made?* What do You see, Father, when You look at me? Sometimes I have a hard time believing that I am made beautifully new in You. But I trust Your promises and Your love. Amen.

And He who sits on the throne said, "Behold, I am making all things new."
REVELATION 21:5 NASB

Prayer Promise #88

One day, you will know Christ fully.

Lord, the more I know about Your creation, the more I marvel. . . .
Your creation is irreducibly complex, multifaceted, and breathtakingly
beautiful—both near and from a distance! And we are only just beginning to understand creation's mysteries. I praise You, Father. I am so
thankful that You are knowable. . .and that one day in heaven, I will know
You fully, completely. Amen.

*The earth will be full of the knowledge of
the Lord as the waters cover the sea.*
ISAIAH 11:9 NASB

Prayer Promise #89

The heavenly Father wants you to look up.

Dear Father, every so often I realize I'm focusing on the pebbles at my feet—on the trivialities of life that trip me up. In these moments, I need Your eyes, Lord. Help me to look up—no matter how rocky the trail I am on. I trust You to help me keep focused on the most important thing—YOU! Amen.

....

....

....

....

....

....

....

....

....

....

....

....

....

Let the rivers clap their hands, let the mountains sing together for joy.
PSALM 98:8 NIV

Prayer Promise #90

The Gospel is alive.

Heavenly Father, whenever I think about sharing my faith, I imagine potential questions—and when I don't have perfect answers for them, that's often enough to keep me from opening my mouth at all. But, Lord, Your Word is clear: we do not convert the lost. The Gospel is alive—and it converts. . .it overtakes. I trust Your Word and its mighty power to do what I cannot. Amen.

*But My words and My statutes, which
I commanded My servants the prophets,
did they not overtake and take hold
of your fathers? So they repented.*
ZECHARIAH 1:6 AMPC

Prayer Promise #91

God invites you to join in an eternal song of praise.

Thank You for music, Father. I hear a symphony in rain dancing on the rooftops and wind blowing through bare tree branches. In the splash of a brook over stones and little children shouting a hymn at the tops of their lungs. Your creation praises You all the time, Father—with every breath and in every moment. Thank You for inviting me into this eternal song of praise! Amen.

....

....

....

....

....

....

....

....

....

Shout joyfully to the LORD,
all the earth; break forth in
song, rejoice, and sing praises.
PSALM 98:4 NKJV

Prayer Promise #92

You can be used by the Lord—just as you are.

Father God, anyone can share Your Good News—even me! You haven't laid out any lofty requirements that I must meet. In fact, You don't even require me to have an answer to every question. The only requirement You do have is simple—I must be saved by the blood of Jesus. I believe, Father. Please give me the courage to share my faith. Amen.

We also believe and therefore speak.
2 CORINTHIANS 4:13 NKJV

Prayer Promise #93

God longs to astonish you with joy!

God, thank You for the gift of laughter. How my soul needs it to lighten my days. When I laugh till my sides ache, it's so good for my soul—it brings a level of contentment that's indescribable. I am grateful for Your miracles that bring laughter and joy: Sarah with news of her unlikely baby; Lazarus raised to life; the disciples with their overflowing catch of fish! You are a true joy-giver! Amen.

....

....

....

....

....

....

....

....

....

....

....

....

*Then our mouth was filled with laughter
and our tongue with joyful shouting.*
PSALM 126:2 NASB

Prayer Promise #94

The Lord will gently nudge you to obey.

Father, I know. . .I am so sorry for putting off what You've been asking of me. While I've tried to forget, You keep bringing it to the forefront of my mind. You've gently prodded and nudged me toward obedience. Tonight, Lord, my spirit is filled with a certainty. . .I am ready to follow Your plan for me. Thank You for strengthening my faith. Amen.

Now faith is the substance of things hoped for, the evidence of things not seen.
HEBREWS 11:1 NKJV

Prayer Promise #95

You have a heavenly Provider.

My Father, my God, my Provider. . .You have always seen to it that my needs are met. When I think about it, I've never been truly self-sufficient at any point in my life. It's a humbling thought! Every human being is a pauper by nature. Everything we have comes from You. Thank You for Your many blessings! Amen.

You open your hand and satisfy
the desires of every living thing.
PSALM 145:16 NIV

Prayer Promise #96

The heavenly Father delights in saying YES!

Father, the people who don't really know You often think of You as a heavenly killjoy—stopping them from doing super fun things that would bring them great enjoyment. But those who know You. . .we know better! Thank You that You do not delight in denial; You delight in saying yes to Your people. I trust You are planning the ultimate celebration—one that will last for eternity. I can't wait! Amen.

They celebrate your abundant goodness
and joyfully sing of your righteousness.
PSALM 145:7 NIV

Prayer Promise #97

You are the heavenly Creator's in-progress piece of art.

Lord, no matter how long I've known You, You promise that You'll continue working in and through me. I am so thankful that even as I make progress, I am not who I used to be. . .and it's all because of You. Thank You for working on me—patiently, lovingly, faithfully. You are the Potter; I am the grateful clay in Your hands. Amen.

....

....

....

....

....

....

....

....

....

....

....

"For the eyes of the Lord are on the righteous and his ears are attentive to their prayer."
1 PETER 3:12 NIV

Prayer Promise #98

The Lord is the Master Weaver,
and He has control over all of life's threads.

Father, sometimes I look at the shape of my life and see disaster; but I know You see it quite differently. You see the tapestry that faces the light, while I see only the chaos and mess that hides in the dark. I appreciate the glimpses You give—when I can see how You're weaving all the threads of my life together. I long for the days when I will see Your handiwork unveiled. Thank You for being the Master Weaver of my life. Amen.

*To the end that my glory may sing praise
to thee, and not be silent. O LORD my God,
I will give thanks unto thee for ever.*
PSALM 30:12 KJV

Prayer Promise #99

The Lord will lead you to a good place.

Heavenly Father, I know that from the very beginning of time, You had the perfect ending in mind. I know I can trust where You are leading me—which is to a very good place. I praise You for the amazing grace that has allowed my story to be a small part of the story You are telling, Lord. Amen.

....

....

....

....

....

....

....

....

....

....

....

He has made everything beautiful in its time. He has also set an eternity in the human heart; yet no one can fathom what God has done from beginning to end.
ECCLESIASTES 3:11 NIV

Prayer Promise #100

The Word of God is unchanging.

Lord, You have preserved Your Word for thousands of years. It is uncorrupted; it is unchanged; it has not been forgotten. You chiseled Your law into rock for Moses, but now Your Word is written into our hearts. And we too will live uncorrupted and unforgotten but, thanks be to You, *changed!* Amen.

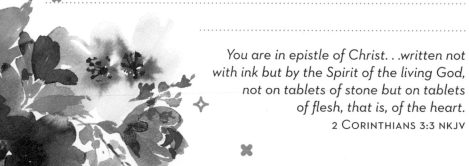

You are in epistle of Christ. . .written not with ink but by the Spirit of the living God, not on tablets of stone but on tablets of flesh, that is, of the heart.
2 CORINTHIANS 3:3 NKJV

Prayer Promise #101

God has always made miracles happen for His people.

Father, I see Your chosen people living in their little land, surrounded by many enemies, and it seems like a situation ripe for disaster. But I know Your Word—and I know You love Your people and won't abandon them. I praise You for how You have protected Israel for thousands of years. You've sent fire from heaven, parted the middle of the sea. . .and there's surely more miracles to come. Thank You, Lord! Amen.

"Who among the gods is like you, LORD?
Who is like you—majestic in holiness,
awesome in glory, working wonders?"
EXODUS 15:11 NIV

Prayer Promise #102

God made you for relationship with others.

Heavenly Father, sometimes I feel like I'd do better on a remote island. It's hard to live in community. My rough edges meet the rough edges of others, and what results are scrapes and sparks and wounds. I can learn so much from Jesus' relationship with the disciples. . .those He ate with, lived with, loved, and traveled with. Jesus is the perfect example of living in community. Thank You, Father! Amen.

Pointing to his disciples, he said, "Here are my mother and my brothers. For whoever does the will of my Father in heaven is my brother and sister and mother."
MATTHEW 12:49–50 NIV

Prayer Promise #103

The Lord is pleased when you remember His faithfulness to you.

Lord, I so easily forget Your faithfulness. Forgive me. The Israelites' path was littered with altars and memorials, their calendar marked with feasts and holidays and fasts—all reminders of Your faithfulness, Father. Please show me tangible ways to remember Your faithfulness to me too. Amen.

....

....

....

....

....

....

....

....

....

....

....

....

Then let us arise and go up to Bethel, and I will make there an altar to God Who answered me in the day of my distress and was with me wherever I went.
GENESIS 35:3 AMPC

Prayer Promise #104

God wants you to give Him more of your time.

Thank You, Lord, for this day—twenty-four precious hours. Some of my hours are spent in sleep, some in work, some in eating, some in talking, some in staring out the kitchen window. . . How many of those hours do I give to You? Thank You for the reminder that relationships require time, and I vow to give You more of each day—each day that is already a gift from You. Amen.

This is the day which the LORD hath made;
we will rejoice and be glad in it.
PSALM 118:24 KJV

Prayer Promise #105

The heavenly Creator promises new life.

Father, after the dead of winter, I am so ready for the beauty of springtime—seeds that spring to life with the warming sun and gentle rain, nests that hold eggs the color of the sky, ponds that sparkle and sing with dragonflies and frogs. Thank You for the promise of spring, for green and new life. And thank You for heaven, where that fleeting green will never fade away. Amen.

"For lo, the winter is past, the rain is over and gone. The flowers appear on the earth; the time of singing has come."
SONG OF SOLOMON 2:11–12 NKJV

Prayer Promise #106

Even ordinary days overflow with holiness.

Help me to be thankful even in the small things, Father. I yearn to see each day as a gift—swathed in sunrise—to be unwrapped. Thank You, Lord, for each moment and remind me that ordinary days are really overflowing with holiness. I am grateful for the gift of ordinary days—and for the gifts I will come to notice as I learn to live in thankfulness. Amen.

For who hath despised the day of small things? for they shall rejoice.
ZECHARIAH 4:10 KJV

Prayer Promise #107

**The Bible is as true and practical today
as it was thousands of years ago.**

God, how many books written millennia ago are still useful today? Curious maybe, or interesting. . .but practical? . . . I can't think of even one. But, Father, Your Word is as true today as when the ink was still wet. It is beautiful. Inspiring. It surprises. It sustains. It transforms. I praise the living Word! Amen.

....

....

....

....

....

....

....

....

....

....

*O LORD, You are my God. I will exalt You,
I will praise Your name, for You have
done wonderful things; Your counsels
of old are faithfulness and truth.*
ISAIAH 25:1 NKJV

Prayer Promise #108

Because of the Cross, death will be swallowed up in victory!

Lord, I awoke this morning feeling sad. . .missing my loved ones who have passed away. Death seems so strange and so wrong. My loved ones are out of sight and out of reach. But, Father, You bring me comfort. Your Word assures me that death was not part of Your plan—and ultimately, it will be swallowed up in victory! My loved ones who knew You will one day wake up and shout for joy! Hallelujah! Amen.

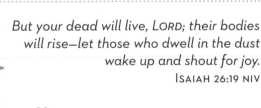

*But your dead will live, Lord; their bodies
will rise—let those who dwell in the dust
wake up and shout for joy.*
Isaiah 26:19 NIV

Prayer Promise #109

Everything in life all comes down to one thing: knowing Christ.

Father God, at the end of the day, it all comes down to knowing You. . . having a relationship with You. Who I am, where I'm going, and what You require of me all depend on who You are. I ask You for a dogged determination to know You better, Lord. Please give me a continual filling of Your Spirit so my eyes and heart are wide open to You. Thank You. Amen.

I've got my eye on the goal, where God is beckoning us onward—to Jesus. I'm off and running, and I'm not turning back.
PHILIPPIANS 3:14 MSG

Prayer Promise #110

Instead of worrying, you should pray.

I praise You, Father, because You are changing me! You are teaching me to take my worries and lift them up to You. . .to trust You with each and every one. I trust You with my life, Lord. I praise You—You are the overcomer; You are my resting place; You are my strength and my fortress. I am so relieved that You are here for me, Lord. Amen.

Don't fret or worry. Instead of worrying, pray. Let petitions and praises shape your worries into prayers, letting God know your concerns.
PHILIPPIANS 4:6 MSG

Prayer Promise #111

Jesus wants us to love just like He loves.

It's easy to love when people behave the way I think they should, Father. But when they don't behave in a way that agrees with me, then I quickly can become apathetic or mean-spirited. Forgive me, Lord. I want to love like You do. Your Spirit, working through my hands, can help me love others no matter how they act. I praise You for that, Lord. Amen.

....

....

....

....

....

....

....

....

....

....

....

....

....

"By this everyone will know that you are my disciples, if you love one another."
JOHN 13:35 NIV

Prayer Promise #112

God protects all things dear
to Him—and that includes you!

Heavenly Father, when I think of how You protect me, I imagine a strong tree—an oak perhaps, or a towering pine—one that will stand, unbowed, through all sorts of weather. I am a small creature padding a hollow in that tree with dry leaves and grasses and curling up in a circle and falling asleep—protected and at peace. Thank You for letting me burrow into Your deep, warm, safe heart, Lord, and remain. Amen.

Keep me as the apple of your eye;
hide me in the shadow of your wings.
Psalm 17:8 NIV

Prayer Promise #113

The Lord wants you to serve without counting the cost.

I do a lot of things for a lot of people, Lord. But today I'm asking You to show me my heart. Am I pleasing You? . . . Am I serving only out of obligation? Or am I serving with the voluntary spirit of my freedom in Christ? I want to serve without counting the cost, Father. Show me who and how You want me to serve. . .in Your holy name. Amen.

"For the LORD searches all hearts and understands all the intent of the thoughts. If you seek Him, He will be found by you."
1 CHRONICLES 28:9 NKJV

Prayer Promise #114

Wherever believers gather in prayer, there is power.

I admit I often struggle working in a group setting, Lord. It's difficult—and I want to do things my way. But Your Word reveals a truth about coming together in prayer with a group of believers: alone in prayer, we are strong; but together in prayer, we are mightier than an army. Help me to join in with joy. Amen.

....

....

....

....

....

....

....

....

....

....

....

Blessed be the LORD, the God of Israel,
from everlasting to everlasting. And all the
people shall say, "Amen." Praise the LORD!
PSALM 106:48 NASB

Prayer Promise #115

The mysteries of God are unending.

Lord, You are the image of the invisible God. You are the Amen, and the "so be it." There is an equation here, the solution just out of my grasp. Jesus equals the image of God, equals Amen, equals "so be it." You are definitely not easy to figure out, Father. I am so thankful that You offer mystery and puzzles and food for thought that will satisfy my soul for eternity. Amen.

....

....

....

....

....

....

....

....

....

....

....

"These are the words of the Amen, the faithful and true witness, the ruler of God's creation."
REVELATION 3:14 NIV

Prayer Promise #116

When you hold your prayers lightly, you allow room for God's will.

Father God, I know what I want, but I can't see the future. I know what I think would be best for me, but I don't have Your eyes. So I pray, but I hold my prayers lightly. Show me Your will and Your way, Lord. Your will be done. Today I will obey and wait on You to act. Amen.

....

....

....

....

....

....

....

....

....

....

....

....

The effective, fervent prayer of a righteous man avails much.
JAMES 5:16 NKJV

Prayer Promise #117

Welcome life's interruptions as a chance to be like Jesus.

Lord, when I attempt to spend quiet time in Your presence, You see the many interruptions that lead to distraction—and sometimes it's irritating. But when I read Your Word, I see that Jesus was often interrupted too. And yet, He never said, "Go away. . .can't you see I'm praying?" Today I will welcome the interruptions as a chance to be more like Jesus. Amen.

Strengthened with all might, according to his glorious power, unto all patience and longsuffering with joyfulness.
Colossians 1:11 kjv

Prayer Promise #118

God wants you to be fully present in the moment.

Father God, Your Word shows Jesus traveling to many different places and interacting with many different people; and yet He never appears to be in a hurry. Jesus was right where He wanted to be in each and every moment...and I long to be more like that, Lord. Please help me slow down and savor each moment You've gifted me. I am here, and so are You! Amen.

"Be still, and know that I am God."
PSALM 46:10 NIV

Prayer Promise #119

Prayer isn't a quick fix for life's problems.

Father, I like quick fixes—amazing tricks that promise to solve my problems fast. But I know You're not like that. Sometimes, a miracle does come—but more often than not, the Christian life is a long haul. What You've shown me clearly, Father, is not to wait for everything to be perfect before I follow You more faithfully. Help me to live each day as though I'm on my knees. Amen.

"Who among all these does not know
that the hand of the LORD has done this,
in whose hand is the life of every living
thing, and the breath of all mankind?"
JOB 12:9–10 NASB

Prayer Promise #120

When you fall, the heavenly Father gives you strength.

I fall, Lord, because I am weak and You are great. And in falling, Your strength miraculously becomes mine. You dwell in me. Your boundless love bears fruit in me: enough to keep and to give away! I—weak, broken, sin-scarred, blind—am strong, whole, pure, clear-eyed, and filled with Your Spirit! Amen.

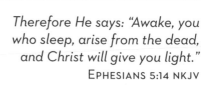

Therefore He says: "Awake, you who sleep, arise from the dead, and Christ will give you light."
Ephesians 5:14 NKJV

Prayer Promise #121

The Lord is faithful.

Heavenly Father, just like the prodigal child, I am still a long way off—far from where You want me to be. Thank You for drawing me closer. I praise You for how Your Word has smoothed the rough, bitter edges of my heart and washed away years of sin and shame. Please help me to drink deeper of Your Word. . .to believe harder that You who promise, are faithful. Amen.

....

....

....

....

....

....

....

....

....

....

"When he was still a great way off,
his father saw him and had compassion,
and ran and fell on his neck and kissed him."
LUKE 15:20 NKJV

Prayer Promise #122

Because of the Cross, your shameful past is forever erased.

Father, You have redeemed my past, and I am so thankful! I've said and done things that I'm not proud of. But You've washed away all my sin and guilt—and I don't have to live in the past. I can face my future with confidence and grace. Amen.

....

....

....

....

....

....

....

....

....

....

....

*As far as the east is from the west,
so far has He removed our
transgressions from us.*
PSALM 103:12 NKJV

Prayer Promise #123

God wants you to make the very best use of your time on earth.

Heavenly Father, the transition of minutes to hours is so incremental that it's tedious to observe. It's certainly easier to focus on large blocks of time than myriad tiny ones. Yet hours are made up of minutes, just like the body is comprised of cells. Each is vital to the whole. Lord, please help me to make the best use of every minute I have. Amen.

....

....

....

....

....

....

....

....

....

....

....

....

Make the most of every opportunity in these evil days.
EPHESIANS 5:16 NLT

Prayer Promise #124

The heavenly Father is the keeper of all resources.

Father, the Bible says You own "the cattle on a thousand hills." You have unlimited resources. So I'm asking You, Father, to supply for my needs today. I know You can remedy any financial situation when it's within Your will. I need Your wisdom, Father. Amen.

"For every animal of the forest is mine, and the cattle on a thousand hills."
PSALM 50:10 NIV

Prayer Promise #125

The Lord will prompt you to share His love with others.

God, I want to be a better witness for You. I have many friends and family members who don't know You. I don't want to be pushy, but I do want to let my light shine. Please open doors for me today—let me sense Your prompting. Thank You, Father. Amen.

....

....

....

....

....

....

....

....

....

....

....

....

....

"Let your light so shine before men, that they may see your good works and glorify your Father in heaven."
MATTHEW 5:16 NKJV

Prayer Promise #126

Satan may be plotting your destruction, but God's power is greater!

I don't want to fall prey to sin because I'm not being careful, Father. Just like guardrails on a dangerous mountain highway, boundaries in my life keep me closer to center and farther away from the cliffs. I know Satan is planning my destruction, but Your power is greater. As long as I'm walking with You, You'll keep me safe. Amen.

....
....
....
....
....
....
....
....
....

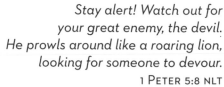

Stay alert! Watch out for your great enemy, the devil. He prowls around like a roaring lion, looking for someone to devour.
1 PETER 5:8 NLT

Prayer Promise #127

God wants you to live with passion and purpose.

Father, I'm in a rut. The monotony of life is wearing away at my sense of purpose right now. But this isn't what You had in mind for my life—not at all! Show me, Lord, how to find meaning in the everyday moments. Open my eyes to the subtle nuances of joy folded into life's sometimes-mundane minutes. I put my life in Your hands. Amen.

In Him we have obtained an inheritance, being predestined according to the purpose of Him who works all things according to the counsel of His will.
EPHESIANS 1:11 NKJV

Prayer Promise #128

You can reflect the joy of Jesus to others by how you live.

Jesus, I believe You enjoyed life immensely. Why else would sinners and tax collectors have wanted to spend time with You? Your mission on earth was sacred and grave; yet, I believe Your demeanor in everyday life was buoyant and pleasant. People loved being in Your presence! Help me learn from Your example, Lord. Let me reflect You in the way I approach living. Amen.

"Be of good cheer, daughter."
MATTHEW 9:22 NKJV

Prayer Promise #129

Some of life's detours are divine appointments.

Father God, being flexible with my day to day routine is difficult for me. I like knowing the plan and the timing of it all. Please help me to realize that some of life's detours are divine appointments—maybe there's someone You need me to meet, or a disaster You want me to avoid. Help me to accept each of the detours that come my way with grace. . .and help me be aware of Your sovereignty over all. Amen.

This is the day the LORD has made;
we will rejoice and be glad in it.
PSALM 118:24 NKJV

Prayer Promise #130

The heavenly Father wants you to live with an eternal perspective.

God, heaven is more than a feel-good fable for the graveside; it's an actual place, as real as this earth and far more lasting. When I live like this earth is the ultimate goal, I tend toward selfish indulgence. When I remember that heaven is my real destination, I put value on lasting things. Remind me to keep a heavenly focus. Amen.

These all died in faith, not having received the promises, but having seen them afar off were assured of them, embraced them and confessed that they were strangers and pilgrims on the earth. For those who say such things declare plainly that they seek a homeland.
HEBREWS 11:13–14 NKJV

Prayer Promise #131

You can trust the love behind the words of Christ.

Lord, I want to have an obedient heart. When I hesitate or postpone what You're telling me to do, that means either I don't trust You or I want my own way—neither of which is good. A child obeys her parents because she acknowledges their right to direct her and because she trusts the love behind their words. Help me, Father, to embrace that kind of attitude when You speak to me. Amen.

....

....

....

....

....

....

....

....

....

....

....

But be doers of the word, and not hearers only, deceiving yourselves.
JAMES 1:22 NKJV

Prayer Promise #132

A relationship with God is the key to contentment.

Father God, I live in a culture that demands more. Wherever I look, I see things I "need." But I know in my heart that accumulating more stuff isn't the path to joy. Your blessings aren't so I can indulge myself, but rather so I can share with others from my abundance. Let my life be marked by a deep contentment that's rooted in You. Amen.

Keep your lives free from the love of money and be content with what you have.
Hebrews 13:5 niv

Prayer Promise #133

God wants you to develop the quality of meekness in your daily life.

Father, I want to develop the characteristic of meekness, a kind of quiet strength. Rather than being a pushover, this trait is a sign of strength. It takes courage to be silent when you want to speak out. Meekness is for those who would be in the forefront of spiritual growth. A life of quiet strength reaps great rewards. Thank You, Lord. Amen.

....

....

....

....

....

....

....

....

....

....

....

*With all lowliness and meekness,
with longsuffering, forbearing
one another in love.*
EPHESIANS 4:2 KJV

Prayer Promise #134

The heavenly Father loves you perfectly, despite your imperfections.

Lord, today I'm discouraged. There are things I see in myself that I really don't like. I feel like I could do so much more for You if it weren't for my flaws. Please help me overcome these issues, or use me despite them. Help me to love and care for myself, as imperfect as I am, and to strive to be the best I can be. Amen.

....

....

....

....

....

....

....

....

....

....

....

*You have searched me,
LORD, and you know me.*
PSALM 139:1 NIV

Prayer Promise #135

God will help you triumph over your insecurities.

Father God, I often find myself comparing my appearance and accomplishments with other women—and this leaves me feeling inadequate and depressed. Although my feelings seem petty and self-centered, they are real to me, Lord. I know this isn't what You have in mind for me. Help me deal with my feelings and give me triumph over them—as I know only You can. Amen.

....

....

....

....

....

....

....

....

....

....

....

I praise you because I am fearfully and wonderfully made.
PSALM 139:14 NIV

Prayer Promise #136

The Lord will help guard your mind.

Heavenly Father, it's so easy to waste time these days on things that don't bring positivity to my life. I need Your help with choosing to spend my free time more wisely—so I don't get caught up in stuff that doesn't feed my soul in some way. Help to guard my mind, Lord, when I select what to listen to and watch. Amen.

For the LORD gives wisdom;
from His mouth come
knowledge and understanding.
PROVERBS 2:6 NKJV

Prayer Promise #137

If you're continually seeking out and reaching out to God in prayer, results will come.

Lord, You tell me to ask and I will receive, to seek and I will find. This sounds too good to be true much of the time. Yet I know You're a giving God whose Word is true. I must not forget that prayer is a way I align my heart better with You. When I'm receptive to Your guiding hand in prayer, I will begin to more clearly see what I should be seeking and asking for—rather than hard-headedly insisting on my desires. I yearn to seek Your will for my life. I will continue knocking. Amen.

....

....

....

....

....

....

....

"Keep on asking, and you will receive what you ask for. Keep on seeking, and you will find. Keep on knocking, and the door will be opened to you. For everyone who asks, receives. Everyone who seeks, finds. And to everyone who knocks, the door will be opened."
MATTHEW 7:7–8 NLT

Prayer Promise #138

The Word of the Lord offers all the love and encouragement you'll ever need.

Father, today I need affirming words. You know that words are important to me. . .and You also know I sometimes struggle with self-worth. The people in my life don't always meet my need to be affirmed verbally, and I can't expect them to fulfill every void in my life. So, Lord, I'm looking to Your Word—it contains all the love and encouragement I need. Thank You. Amen.

....

....

....

....

....

....

....

....

....

....

....

....

A word fitly spoken is like apples of gold in settings of silver.
PROVERBS 25:11 NKJV

Prayer Promise #139

The Lord will take your hand and teach you to trust Him.

Heavenly Father, please teach my heart to trust You fully. I know this is an area of weakness for me. Even though I know Your character and Your track record, it's difficult for me to relinquish the important areas of my life to You. Take my hand. . .teach me. You're the Master; I'm forever Your student. Amen.

....

....

....

....

....

....

....

....

....

....

....

....

I have put my trust in the Lord GOD,
that I may declare all Your works.
PSALM 73:28 NKJV

Prayer Promise #140

God can lead you through a person, a thought, a scripture. . .

Father God, it's so hard to know Your will sometimes. You don't write specific instructions in the sky or emblazon them on a marquee. So how can I know what You want me to do? How can I keep from making a big mistake? Today, please give me wisdom. Please send me Your guidance—through a person, a thought, a scripture. Let me sense Your leading. I want my life to honor Your plan for me. Amen.

If any of you lacks wisdom, you should ask God, who gives generously to all without finding fault, and it will be given to you.
JAMES 1:5 NIV

Prayer Promise #141

The key to true and lasting joy is surrender to Christ.

God, I know there is an area of my life that I always try to rule—all by myself. And this never ends well. I know You need the keys to every room in my heart, and so here I am. . .giving You permission to change, clean out, and add things that are needed. Thank You for showing me the way to lasting joy. Amen.

But now, O Lord, You are our Father;
we are the clay, and You are our potter;
and all we are the work of Your hand.
Isaiah 64:8 NKJV

Prayer Promise #142

**God will give you the grace and strength
you need to run your race with endurance.**

Lord, I recognize that the Christian life requires endurance. It isn't enough to start well. I know difficulties will come; I've faced some already. This brings the words of "Amazing Grace" to mind: "Through many dangers, toils, and snares, I have already come. 'Tis grace that brought me safe thus far, and grace will lead me home." Amen.

*Let us run with endurance the
race that is set before us.*
HEBREWS 12:1 NKJV

Prayer Promise #143

Maturing in Christ takes time.

Father God, so many things in this world are instantaneous. From fast food to instant credit, I can satisfy my penchant for immediate gratification at every juncture. But I need to remind myself that You often work by process. You use the steady maturing of Your Word in me to make me more like Jesus. You, the Master Gardener, water the seeds, prune the unnecessary limbs, and watch over me carefully as the fruit of my life continues to ripen. I aim to revel in Your timely and tender loving care. Amen.

But grow in grace, and in the knowledge of our Lord and Saviour Jesus Christ.
2 PETER 3:18 KJV

Prayer Promise #144

The heavenly Father wants you to be less critical of others.

Dear Lord, criticism can be hurtful. Sometimes people paraphrase Your Word (Matthew 7:1) as "Don't judge." But it really means, "Don't judge unless you want to be judged." When we criticize others, Lord, we open ourselves to the same kind of scrutiny. Help me to become less critical. Thank You. Amen.

....

....

....

....

....

....

....

....

....

....

....

Set a guard over my mouth, LORD;
keep watch over the door of my lips.
PSALM 141:3 NIV

Prayer Promise #145

God will turn things meant for evil into good.

Father God, bitterness can take over and slowly squeeze out life. I don't want to be consumed by bitterness. Help me to let go of the injustices I've experienced and to accept Your healing touch. I want to let go of the bitterness that threatens to take root in my soul. I trust You to take things meant for evil and turn them into good. Thank You, Father. Amen.

....

....

....

....

....

....

....

....

....

....

....

Let all bitterness, wrath, anger, clamor, and evil speaking be put away from you, with all malice.
EPHESIANS 4:31 NKJV

Prayer Promise #146

When you're struggling, you can rely on God to increase your faith.

God, faith is such a delicate concept, yet so mighty in its power. Faith isn't something I can wrap my arms around—but it is something I can rest my soul in. Faith is sometimes trivialized in this world, but I know it's of utmost importance to You. Please increase my faith, Lord. In Your name, amen.

....
....
....
....
....
....
....
....
....
....
....

Now faith is the substance of things hoped for, the evidence of things not seen.
HEBREWS 11:1 KJV

Prayer Promise #147

God will help you hold together the pieces of your busy life.

Father, I have an endless to-do list. There is always someone who needs me. . .and constant demands are on my energy and sanity. I go through life in a state of perpetual exhaustion. While there are responsibilities that I can't ignore—at the same time, Lord, You want me to care for my health. Show me what I can change today. Show me how I can attain emotional and physical wellness so I can be my best self. Amen.

He gives power to the weak, and to those who have no might He increases strength. . . . Those who wait on the LORD shall renew their strength; they shall mount up with wings like eagles, they shall run and not be weary, they shall walk and not faint.
ISAIAH 40:29, 31 NKJV

Prayer Promise #148

The heavenly Father values your tears.

I've heard, Father, that tears speak their own language. If that's true, then You made women verbal in two ways: with words and tears. I cry for a variety of reasons—and sometimes for no reason at all. But since You understand my heart, Lord, You know. Thank You for valuing my tears. Amen.

....
....
....
....
....
....
....
....
....
....
....
....

Put my tears into Your bottle;
are they not in Your book?
PSALM 56:8 NKJV

Prayer Promise #149

God provides help to control your anger.

Father God, I need a solution for my anger. Sometimes I let it take over and then later regret what I've said or done. As I pray and study and grow closer to You, show me ways I can control my anger. Guide me to the right verses to memorize and incorporate into my life. Lead me to someone who can keep me accountable. And most of all, help me strive for self-control. Amen.

If it is possible, as much as depends on you, live peaceably with all men. Beloved, do not avenge yourselves, but rather give place to wrath; for it is written, "Vengeance is Mine, I will repay," says the Lord.
ROMANS 12:18–19 NKJV

Prayer Promise #150

It's possible to live a
worry-free, fear-free life.

Father, peace is an elusive emotion. So many people talk about peace, but few can actually claim it. You promised to give me Your peace—a calm assurance that You are present and sovereign in every moment of my life. I want more of Your peace every day. No matter what upsetting things may happen, Lord, Your peace will help me cope with them all. Thank You. Amen.

"Peace I leave with you,
My peace I give to you."
JOHN 14:27 NKJV

Prayer Promise #151

You can exchange your stress
for the heavenly Father's strength.

Lord, because it has become so overused, the word "stress" hardly affects us; but the effects of stress never fade. I'm facing some stress today, Father. Help me deal with it appropriately. Let me not take it out on my friends, family, or coworkers. I want to leave it all to You—in exchange for Your strength, which will ultimately bring me peace. Amen.

Praise be to the Lord, to God our Savior,
who daily bears our burdens.
PSALM 68:19 NIV

Prayer Promise #152

The heavenly Father knows you better than anyone else.

Father, I'm lonely today. There's no one in my life with whom I feel comfortable sharing my thoughts and feelings right now. I feel like no one really understands me, and this makes me incredibly sad. Remind me, Lord, that You created me—and in so doing, You know me like no one else does or ever will. Help me to feel Your presence. I'm grateful for Your constant love and care. Amen.

God has said, "Never will I leave you;
never will I forsake you."
HEBREWS 13:5 NIV

Prayer Promise #153

According to Christ's heavenly plan, pain will one day be a thing of the past.

Father, this world can sometimes turn on us and cause us terrible pain. Some people blame You for these events; but they couldn't be more wrong. You planned perfection, but human beings messed it up by allowing sin to enter our planet. Thank You for the promise that one day there will be a new earth. Pain will be a thing of the past when we're celebrating in eternity with You. Amen.

We know that the whole creation has been groaning as in the pains of childbirth right up to the present time.
ROMANS 8:22 NIV

Prayer Promise #154

God will give you the words when you aren't sure what to say.

Father God, when I have a friend who's hurting, I often don't know what to say. I don't want to appear superficial or unfeeling. . .and I certainly don't want to be insensitive or melodramatic. Father, please give me the words and guide me as I speak. I want to minister to my hurting friend today. Amen.

. . . who comforts us in all our troubles, so that we can comfort those in any trouble with the comfort we ourselves receive from God.
2 Corinthians 1:4 niv

Prayer Promise #155

God's fingerprint is on every frozen crystal that falls to earth in winter.

Father, the snow is so beautiful. There is something so magical and mesmerizing about the first snowfall each year. I thank You, Lord, for creating this beauty. Each snowflake, unique in design, is a testament to Your greatness in things both big and small. Your creation makes my heart happy. Amen.

He gives snow like wool;
He scatters the frost like ashes.
PSALM 147:16 NKJV

Prayer Promise #156

**Trees are majestic tributes to
Christ's heavenly splendor.**

Father, so much more than branches to climb, shade to enjoy, and logs to burn—trees make such a difference in the landscape. They add beauty and protection. . .and they also convey deep truths. They display what a Christian should be like—rooted deep, connected to a source, full of life, bearing fruit, and standing strong in the storms. Thank You, Father, for trees. Amen.

*And he shall be like a tree
planted by the rivers of water.*
PSALM 1:3 KJV

Prayer Promise #157

God cares even about one lonely sparrow.

Father, Your Word says that not even one sparrow falls to the ground without Your notice. And so, how much more do You care for me? I revel in this truth: I am worthy in Your sight! I don't have to try to get Your attention, because I am already important to You! Thank You for reminding me that I'm valued and loved. Amen.

....

....

....

....

....

....

....

....

....

....

Are not two sparrows sold for a penny?
Yet not one of them will fall to the
ground outside your Father's care. . . .
So don't be afraid; you are worth
more than many sparrows.
MATTHEW 10:29, 31 NIV

Prayer Promise #158

You won't always get the
answers to your "why" questions.

Sometimes, Father, I'm like a child. I want to know why. But You don't always give an answer. You know that with my human understanding, I can't comprehend Your sovereign ways or grasp the purpose behind Your decisions. Truthfully, there are some things that I'm better off not knowing. Help me to be content and trust You to run the universe. Amen.

"The secret things belong to the LORD our God, but those things which are revealed belong to us and to our children forever."
DEUTERONOMY 29:29 NKJV

Prayer Promise #159

God's plans aren't your plans— and His plans are always better!

Father, today I found my life on a detour. I'm on a path I didn't bargain for . . .and I'm not so sure I like it. This wasn't part of my plan. What are You doing in my life, Lord? Why is this happening? This situation definitely makes no sense to my earthly mind—but I choose to trust You. Please bless me with perseverance and patience. I'm going to need them while I wait for You to show me what's next. Amen.

....

....

....

....

....

....

....

....

....

....

And we know that in all things God works for the good of those who love him, who have been called according to his purpose.
ROMANS 8:28 NIV

Prayer Promise #160

God has a promise for every season, event, and emotion in your life.

The Bible is overflowing with Your promises, Lord. Believers of every age have stood firm on Your promises and had the strength to weather temptation, face persecution, endure grief, and triumph over every obstacle they encountered. Thank You for filling the passages of scripture with such beautiful assurances of Your presence and power and love. I am so blessed! Amen.

....

....

....

....

....

....

....

....

....

....

....

He has given us his very great
and precious promises.
2 PETER 1:4 NIV

Read through the Bible in a Year Plan

1/1	Gen. 1-3	1/25	Exod. 19-20
1/2	Gen. 4:1-7:9	1/26	Exod. 21-23
1/3	Gen. 7:10-10:32	1/27	Exod. 24-27
1/4	Gen. 11-14	1/28	Exod. 28-29
1/5	Gen. 15-18	1/29	Exod. 30-31
1/6	Gen. 19-21	1/30	Exod. 32-33
1/7	Gen. 22-24	1/31	Exod. 34-35
1/8	Gen. 25-27	2/1	Exod. 36-38
1/9	Gen. 28-29	2/2	Exod. 39-40
1/10	Gen. 30-31	2/3	Lev. 1-4
1/11	Gen. 32-34	2/4	Lev. 5-7
1/12	Gen. 35-36	2/5	Lev. 8-10
1/13	Gen. 37-39	2/6	Lev. 11-12
1/14	Gen. 40-41	2/7	Lev. 13:1-14:32
1/15	Gen. 42-43	2/8	Lev. 14:33-15:33
1/16	Gen. 44-45	2/9	Lev. 16-17
1/17	Gen. 46-48	2/10	Lev. 18-20
1/18	Gen. 49-50	2/11	Lev. 21-23
1/19	Exod. 1-3	2/12	Lev. 24-25
1/20	Exod. 4-6	2/13	Lev. 26-27
1/21	Exod. 7-9	2/14	Num. 1-2
1/22	Exod. 10-12	2/15	Num. 3-4
1/23	Exod. 13-15	2/16	Num. 5-6
1/24	Exod. 16-18	2/17	Num. 7